GW01376891

Pre-1914 Cla
Two G̶o̶t̶h̶i̶c̶ Tales

Mary Green

Folens
Publishers

BODMIN
COMMUNITY COLLEGE
CORNWALL

L479924

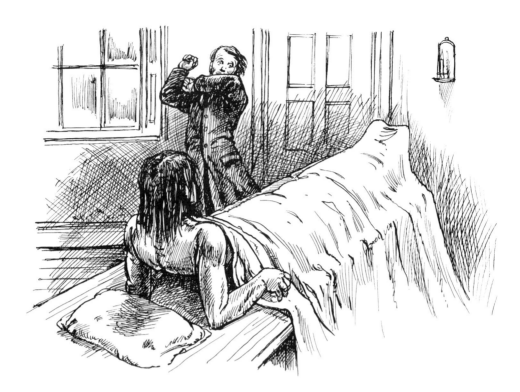

Acknowledgements

Folens allows photocopying of pages marked 'copiable page' for educational use, providing that this use is within the confines of the purchasing institution. Copiable pages should not be declared in any return in respect of any photocopying licence.

Folens books are protected by international copyright laws. All rights are reserved. The copyright of all materials in this book, except where otherwise stated, remains the property of the publisher and authors. No part of this publication may be reproduced, stored in a retrieval system, or transmitted, in any form or by any means, for whatever purpose, without the written permission of Folens Limited.

Mary Green hereby asserts her moral right to be identified as the author of this work in accordance with the Copyright, Designs and Patents Act 1988.

Editor: Alison MacTier
Cover design: Ed Gallagher and Gary Ward
Cover image: *Mary Shelley's Frankenstein*
© Tristar (Colombia). Image supplied by The BFI.

Layout artist: Philippa Jarvis
Illustrations: Jeffrey Burn – Graham-Cameron Illustration

'Lady Lazarus' in *Ariel* by Sylvia Plath reproduced by permission of the publishers, Faber and Faber Limited. 'Makers and Creatures' in *The Black and White Days* by Vernon Scannell reproduced by permission of the publishers, Robson Books. 'The Ratcatcher' by Roald Dahl taken from *Someone Like You*. Extract reproduced by permission of the publishers, Penguin Books Ltd. Extract from *An Outline of English Literature* edited by Pat Rogers, published by Oxford University Press. Extract from *The Portable Poe*, edited by Van Doren Stern, published by Penguin Books Ltd.

© 2000 Folens Limited, on behalf of the author.

Every effort has been made to contact copyright holders of material used in this book. If any have been overlooked, we will be pleased to make any necessary arrangements.

First published 2000 by Folens Limited, Dunstable and Dublin.

Folens Limited, Albert House, Apex Business Centre, Boscombe Road, Dunstable, LU5 4RL, United Kingdom.

ISBN 1 84163 511 1

Contents

Teachers' notes

The writers, their lives and times: Mary Shelley; Edgar Allan Poe (Pages 6–14)

These pages cover aspects of the writers' biographies, the literary influences, the historical and cultural periods and two chronologies, one for each writer, outlining published works and important historical events.

Key Events

Summary of events: *Frankenstein* (Page 15); 'The Black Cat' (Page 36)

These pages give an outline of the main events and can be retained by students. In *Frankenstein*, they do not include references to chapters, but are organised according to who is relating the story. Throughout this publication, all text references are made to chapters, rather than volumes, for ease of access.

Recording key events: *Frankenstein* (Page 16); 'The Black Cat' (Page 37)

The timelines can be used to record key events and other important features, such as those related to structure and language use.

Frankenstein

Characters (Pages 17–20)

The following characters are covered: Victor Frankenstein, the monster, Robert Walton and Elizabeth Frankenstein.

Who's who? – other characters (Page 21)

This sheet gives useful information on some of the numerous minor characters in *Frankenstein*. Most show little or no development. Those selected appear most often or are active in the plot in some way. The sheet can be kept as reference.

Who says? (Page 22)

Students are asked to identify the speaker, what is being discussed and where it occurs.

Language, style and structure

Beginning and end (Page 23)

Extracts from two of Robert Walton's letters, taken from the beginning and end of the novel are provided to illustrate the epistolary novel. Students are asked to identify the difference in tone between the two letters and to write about the way in which Robert Walton's story mirrors Victor's.

Telling the story 1 and 2 (Pages 24 and 25)

The narrative is told in a complex way in *Frankenstein*. Page 24 gives information about the different narrative voices and their relationships and should be used to identify who is speaking in the quotations on page 25. Students are also asked to write about whether or not Victor's account is reliable.

The language of the Gothic novel (Page 26)

The quality of language in *Frankenstein* varies. While the monster is often eloquent, some of the descriptions are verbose and repetitive. Students are asked to

decide which of the extracts they prefer and why.

Making connections; The modern Prometheus (Pages 27–28)

The use of allusion in the novel is discussed here. On page 27, students are asked to identify Coleridge's *The Ancient Mariner* and also to think of modern-day allusions to *Frankenstein*. Page 28 deals with the main allusion in the novel, the Greek myth of Prometheus. Students are required to make connections between the myth and the novel.

On screen (Page 29)

Kenneth Branagh's 1994 film, *Mary Shelley's Frankenstein* is discussed and students are given opportunities to compare the book with the film.

Themes

The monster: what am I? (Page 30)

The monster pervades the novel as character, symbol and theme. Students are asked to rank statements about the monster in order of importance and to identify and write about the most important.

Playing God (Page 31)

Here, the continued appeal of *Frankenstein* and its relationship to modern scientific development is explored. (You may also wish to discuss the relationship of *Frankenstein* to the science-fiction novel, as well as the horror story.)

The Doppelgänger (Page 32)

The 'double' is explored on this sheet and students are asked to examine the two sides of Victor's personality, the monster being his 'other' side.

Victims and crimes (Page 33)

Most characters are either victims or they commit injustices. Students are given a table to complete that asks them to consider why this might be.

Outcast (Page 34)

The theme of alienation is discussed and students are required to write notes explaining why particular characters are alienated.

Other themes (Page 35)

A series of minor themes are presented on this page. Students should identify what they are and find examples of them in the novel. (You may feel that some are more important than those mentioned on previous pages.)

'The Black Cat'

Characters (Pages 38–40)

Here, the narrator, Pluto and the narrator's wife are covered. These activity sheets allow students to record useful details. They can be kept as study aids.

Key quotations (Page 41)

This sheet involves identifying three important quotations from the story and their significance. Students should add others of their own choice and keep them for reference.

Teachers' notes

Language, style and structure

The narrative voice (Page 42)
Features of the narrative voice are given and students are asked to tick those that they agree with. They are then asked to write about whether or not the voice should be trusted.

Symbols (Page 43)
Several symbols from the story are depicted and an explanation of what they mean is required.

Poe's use of language (Page 44)
This sheet involves the extract in which the narrator gives motives for his actions which the students are asked to annotate and interpret.

Climaxes (Page 45)
Students are asked to identify the main and other climaxes and to write brief notes about what is happening in each one.

Features of the Gothic tale (Page 46)
Typical features of the Gothic tale are given for students to record examples from 'The Black Cat' along with other relevant points. An example is provided.

Themes

Madness (Page 47)
This page deals with the opening paragraph of the story. An interpretation is given, outlining its contradictions. Students discuss the theme of madness and decide whether or not the opening paragraph is ironic. (A definition of irony is given, but you may wish to discuss this further.)

The divided personality (Page 48)
Students are given an extract describing the narrator's character as a child and in early manhood and asked to contrast it with his subsequent behaviour.

The supernatural (Page 49)
The supernatural (manifested as the black cat) is discussed here as representing the psychological breakdown of a character and the narrator's inability (by the end of the tale) to take responsibility for his actions. Students are asked to decide and write about what else the black cat represents.

Stepping over the boundaries (Page 50)
Transgression, a common theme in stories of the fantastic, is discussed. Students are asked to consider modern day examples and to write about why they think the narrator commits such crimes. (This sheet can be linked to 'Poe's use of language', page 44, in which the narrator gives motives for his actions.)

Wider reading
These pages give a range of approaches to the comparison of texts written before and after 1900, taking into account the different historical and cultural periods.

'Lady Lazarus' and 'The Black Cat'; 'Lady Lazarus' (Pages 51, 52, 53)
This includes Sylvia Plath's poem 'Lady Lazarus', along with suggestions for an assignment that compares the themes and language of the poem with those in 'The Black Cat'.

Lennie (Page 54)
Suggestions are given for writing an assignment in which a comparison is made between Lennie from John Steinbeck's *Of Mice and Men* and the monster in *Frankenstein*.

The outsider (Page 55)
Here, suggestions are given for looking at the theme of alienation in *Daz 4 Zoe* by Robert Swindells and *Frankenstein*.

The act of creation; 'Makers and Creatures' (Pages 56, 57)
'Makers and creatures', a poem by Vernon Scannell, is made available along with suggestions for drawing parallels between it and *Frankenstein*. Suggestions for a more complex assignment are also given.

'The Ratcatcher' and 'The Black Cat'; 'The Ratcatcher' (Pages 58, 59)
Students are asked to explore the similarities and differences in the way horror is created between Roald Dahl's story and 'The Black Cat'.

Exam and essay practice

Frankenstein: Who is the monster? (Page 60)
The popular description of the monster as 'Frankenstein' and the reasons for this are explored. The story has been depicted in many different ways, through a variety of media, and the students should be aware of some of these. The most important point they should note is the shift in the popular imagination of Victor Frankenstein – from the monster to the villain (the monster is frequently given the name 'Frankenstein').

'The Black Cat': Uncertainty (Page 62)
The issue outlined here deals with those features of the supernatural that create a sense of unreliability in the mind of the reader. Students should be clear that we are not discussing 'reality' in the literal sense, but rather the issue of whether or not the reader agrees to suspend disbelief.

Useful questions: *Frankenstein*, 'The Black Cat' (Pages 61, 63)
These sheets require some understanding of the historical period in which the authors were writing as well as an understanding of the texts.

Answers

Selected answers (Page 64)
This sheet provides answers relating to questions on selected activity sheets.

Mary Shelley

Parents and early life

Mary Shelley was born on 30 August 1797 in London and named Mary Godwin. Her father, William Godwin, was a well-known freethinker and radical (he did not follow the established view). He had come from an uneducated background but had developed his own ideas under the influence of the freethinkers of the time. Her mother, the feminist Mary Wollstonecraft, wrote *A Vindication of the Rights of Women* (1792) and died ten days after her daughter's birth. Mary also left behind a daughter, Fanny Imlay, by a relationship with an American. After her death, Fanny, the young Mary and William Godwin formed the household.

In 1801, when Mary was four years old, William Godwin married Mary Jane Clairmont. The relationship between his daughter and his new wife was difficult. Perhaps the young child resented the presence of a new mother, for although she never knew her own daughter, Mary Wollstonecraft had left a profound impression on her. Mary Jane Clairmont already had two children and so the family grew from three members to six and then to seven when she and William Godwin had a son.

Mary Godwin was an attractive child and the most able in the family. The children were mainly educated at home and encouraged to read. There were opportunities to listen to and perhaps discuss the issues and concerns of the day with well-known intellectuals. By the time Mary met the poet Percy Bysshe Shelley when she was sixteen, she would have begun to form her own opinions.

Meeting Shelley

Percy Bysshe Shelley was a radical aged about twenty when he became a friend of William Godwin. He and his wife Harriet visited the Godwin home to talk and exchange ideas. However, Percy had fallen out of love with his wife by 1814 and he developed a relationship with the young Mary. In the summer of that year, they eloped, much to her father's annoyance and Harriet's distress. Events over the next two years moved quickly. Mary and Percy travelled to the continent with Mary's stepsister Claire Clairmont and returned to England a few months later. Harriet, who was pregnant at the time, gave birth to Shelley's child in November. Mary, in the following February (of 1815), gave birth to his daughter who died a few days later. By the end of the year she was pregnant again and in 1816 she gave birth to a son, William Shelley. In the same year, Fanny Imlay committed suicide and Harriet, Shelley's wife, took her own life. She was found drowned in the Serpentine.

- Write down what indications there are that Mary Shelley might have drawn on her own family experiences when she wrote *Frankenstein*.

Mary Shelley (continued)

Marriage and later life

Mary and Shelley married soon after Harriet's death and William Godwin and Mary were reconciled. The Shelleys were often in financial difficulties but they took a house, Albion House, close to London in Great Marlow, where Mary completed *Frankenstein*. In 1817, the Shelleys had another child, Clara, and in 1818 the family travelled to Italy. This was partly for Shelley's health and partly to see Byron, a close friend. Among the party were Claire Clairmont and her child Allegra, Byron's daughter. It is supposed that this visit

was an attempt to encourage him to take some responsibility for Allegra. There is also strong evidence that Shelley and Claire were lovers. Shelley believed in free love and the two were close. Other matters were to take precedence, however. Clara, who was a sickly child, died near Venice and Mary blamed Shelley for neglecting her and the child. The following year, in 1818, their son William died near Rome and in 1819 Percy was born, the only Shelley child to survive to adulthood. In 1822, Mary had a miscarriage but was saved by the prompt action of her husband, who had some understanding of anatomy. Then Shelley himself was drowned three years later in a boating accident while sailing from Leghorn to Spezia.

Shelley was given to wild fancies. He was sometimes hysterical, sometimes suicidal but was also exciting and was full of ideas and fine poetry. Mary Shelley would have had an interesting life with him but a distressing one too. She never married again and suffered from depression, which was hardly surprising, given her experiences. The rest of her life was spent as an independent woman, bringing up Percy and earning a living by writing. She returned to England in 1823, where she died in 1851 at the age of fifty-three.

Writing

Mary Shelley began work on *Frankenstein* in 1816 while she was in the company of Shelley, Byron and others in the French Alps. The group probably discussed poetry, science and a range of ideas. (This may well have included discussions of Luigi Galvani's experiments with electricity and the movement of muscles in animals. Shelley was interested in 'galvanism'.) Each decided to write a ghost story for amusement and this was how Mary Shelley came to write the basis of *Frankenstein*. It was an extraordinary feat for a young woman of eighteen. Ellen Moers, in her book *Literary Women* (1978) stresses that Victor Frankenstein defies death not by extending his own life but by 'giving birth' to a new one. She refers to the 'Female Gothic' (Gothic writing by women). None of Mary Shelley's subsequent novels or short stories carried as much impact but she continued to write in various forms, particularly biographies, and edited Shelley's poems and letters. Among her most interesting novels are: *Valperga* (1823) set in the fourteenth century and concerned with self-interest and ambition; *The Last Man* (1826) set in the twenty-first century where the plague has killed the population; and *Mathilda* – a tale of incest which was not published until after her death.

● Although Mary Shelley was influenced by Shelley and other male writers, in what way is *Frankenstein* a 'female' novel? Do you agree with Ellen Moers?

Edgar Allan Poe

Edgar Allan Poe was born in Boston on 19 January 1809. Both his parents were actors. His father had deserted the family and his mother had died by the time Poe was two. He was cared for by a wealthy tobacco exporter John Allan and his wife. They lived in Richmond, Virginia, in the Southern states. The family moved to England in 1815 where Edgar attended school until 1820. They returned to Richmond where he attended two more schools. It would seem that Edgar was a sensitive boy who was ill-suited to the character of the stern John Allan and this, along with frequent disruption, meant his childhood was an unhappy one.

Youth and middle life

In 1826 Poe attended the University of Virginia but was removed because he spent his time drinking and gambling. His relationship with John Allan became worse and he was given only a small allowance to live on. However, in 1827, at the age of eighteen, he published his first book of poems *Tamerlane and other Poems*. He also joined the army as a private, where he rose to the rank of sergeant-major before leaving in 1829. His second book of poems *Al Aaraaf* was published in the same year but he was still short of money and, in 1831, he went to live with his aunt, Mrs Maria Clemm, in Baltimore where he stayed for four years. He married her thirteen-year-old daughter, Virginia, in 1836. During this period, he worked on the *Southern Literary Messenger* as an editorial assistant. Both his drinking and his ideas often met with disapproval and cost him his job more than once. Despite living in the North, Poe saw himself as a Southerner, 'allied to the slave-owning class'. He inherited no money from the Allans and had financial difficulties all his life. He, his wife and aunt moved from place to place in poverty and Poe worked for several magazines to earn a living. However, he did manage to publish 'The Narrative of Arthur Gordon Pym' (1838) and many well-known stories such as 'The Fall of the House of Usher' (1839) and 'The Black Cat' (1843).

The last years

In 1842, Virginia became seriously ill, dying finally of tuberculosis in 1847. This had a deep effect on Poe, who always needed female support. Although he buried himself in work and made attempts to marry again, he also drank heavily and died from what appears to have been alcoholism on 7 October 1849. He was only forty years old.

- Discuss with a friend: What evidence is there in 'The Black Cat' that Poe might have drawn on his own experiences?

Edgar Allan Poe (continued)

Poe wrote almost continuously. He wrote poetry, criticism (what he called 'Opinions'), letters, a short novel and different kinds of tales of fantasy.

His stories of Mystery and Ratiocination (deduction) such as the 'Murders in the Rue Morgue' (1841) with the central character, the detective Auguste Dupin, are considered to be an early form of the detective novel. This has heavily influenced other writers that followed. Here, feelings and hunches are important. This is also true of stories such as 'The Black Cat'.

Poe's poetry, like his tales, creates mystery and tension and there is great skill in his rhyme, metre and imagery. 'The Raven' (1845), a narrative poem in eighteen verses, has considerable power and is still popular today. Here is the first verse.

> Once upon a midnight dreary, while I pondered, weak and weary,
> Over many a quaint and curious volume of forgotten lore –
> While I nodded, nearly napping, suddenly there came a tapping,
> As of some one gently rapping – rapping at my chamber door
> "'Tis some visitor," I muttered, "tapping at my chamber door –
> Only this and nothing more."

Poe's 'Opinions' show clearly what he felt a writer should write. He felt that works of art should stimulate the heart, rather than the mind; feeling rather than judgement. They should affect the reader directly. They should create atmosphere and provoke the imagination. Even in his detective stories, this is true.

- Read 'The Raven' and other short stories by Poe. What similarities do you notice between them?

The Gothic period

Although different in several ways, both *Frankenstein* and 'The Black Cat' are Gothic stories. The Gothic style was fashionable in the eighteenth and nineteenth centuries and has been revived in the twentieth century too. It influenced writers, architects and other artists. It also has links with the medieval period and is most obvious in the architecture of the twelfth and thirteenth centuries.

Many great cathedrals and abbeys were built in Europe in the Gothic style. These were magnificent, dramatic buildings, highly decorated and with pointed arches. The interiors were towering spaces with contrasts of light and shadow. Later, however, the power of the monasteries declined and, after the French Revolution, monastic orders were abolished in France. Consequently, many churches and abbeys all over Europe fell into disrepair.

The appeal of the Gothic at the time that Mary Shelley and Edgar Allan Poe were writing was related to the historical period and shifts in attitudes and beliefs. Feeling and emotion rather than reason and judgement became important. This was also a feature of the Romantic movement to which the Gothic novel is linked. The typical Gothic tale emphasises the supernatural, horror, mystery, dramatic landscapes, secret places, ruins and intensity of feeling. The first Gothic tale to be written was *The Castle of Otranto* (1765) by Hugh Walpole and had a pseudo-medieval setting. The most popular novelist became Ann Radcliffe who wrote such novels as *The Mysteries of Udolpho* (1794) and *The Romance of the Forest* (1791). Gothic novels are also concerned with following one's desires, breaking or challenging rules and ideas, and with imprisonment. They can deal with madness, dreams and nightmares and they use, 'the medieval setting of castle and convent, in their ugly aspect as prisons, physical and emotional'.

● Make brief notes on the following:

   a. What connections can you see between the Gothic during the medieval period and the eighteenth- and nineteenth-century Gothic novel?

   b. Why can we call *Frankenstein* or 'The Black Cat' Gothic tales?

   c. What examples of the Gothic can you think of that exist today? Why do you think the Gothic continues to appeal?

 © Folens (copiable page)

The Romantic movement

During the eighteenth century, the concern with feeling and imagination became important. It was a reaction both against the emphasis on logic and order that was dominant at the time and also against the established institutions. This concern with emotions affected all kinds of art: poetry, the novel, drama and painting, but it is probably true to say that it reached its height in poetry. William Wordsworth, Samuel Taylor Coleridge and William Blake (who was also a painter and an engraver) are the older generation of Romantics. Percy Bysshe Shelley (husband of Mary Shelley), Lord Byron and John Keats were the principal poets of the younger generation.

Many of them, such as Shelley and Blake, had strong political views and reacted passionately against such issues as the slave trade and the condition of the poor, particularly in the growing cities where industrialisation was becoming more and more evident. They were interested in human rights. Shelley, for example, was greatly influenced by Thomas Paine who wrote *The Rights of Man* (1791). They also valued nature in its wildness, reacting against the idea of human intervention. Blake's well-known *Songs of Innocence and Experience* (1789) reveal this.

Of course, not all those who were influenced by the Romantics shared all their attitudes. People took what they liked from these ideas and used them for their own ends. Some emphasised feeling and imagination and forgot about human rights. Some exaggerated feeling and imagination and took it into the realms of fantasy and horror. The Gothic novel is an example of this. But there is no doubt that the Romantics had a profound effect that is still felt today. We talk about people responding with their 'heart' rather than their 'head' and there are many popular political issues that can be traced back to the Romantics.

1. Make a list of any examples you can think of today that show the influence of the Romantics. Think about popular political issues as well as any novels or writing you know.

2. Make notes on the way the Gothic novel links to the Romantic period. Try to think of more than one link in the works of the author you are studying.

The historical period

Britain and Europe

The eighteenth and nineteenth centuries saw great social and political upheaval. The American colonies revolted and gained independence. There was revolution in France. There was fear of revolution in Britain by those in power and joy at the prospect by radicals such as William Godwin and Percy Bysshe Shelley. Political pamphlets were distributed and ideas were discussed in coffee houses. There was also war between France and England, ending in 1815 with the Battle of Waterloo. Great changes between the town and the countryside were seen. Industrialisation meant that towns and cities grew. Communications improved but life for the poor remained harsh or became harsher. Scientific developments went hand in hand with the industrial revolution. James Watt invented the steam engine in 1784 and, a year later, Edmund Cartwright invented the power loom, which was used in mills and factories. With this also came the fear by workers that machines would replace jobs. The Luddite riots of 1811 saw machines smashed in violent reaction. This furthered the idea of revolution. As the nineteenth century progressed, greater numbers of ordinary people created organised groups fighting for workers' rights and in 1825 trades unions were legalised. In 1832, the Reform Bill was passed. While this meant that greater numbers of the middle classes gained the right to vote, the working classes gained nothing. A 'People's Charter' (a list of rights) was drawn up in 1842 and ignored by parliament, leading to further riots. Gradually the general population gained the right to vote (although it would not be until the twentieth century that this included women).

The United States of America

The eighteenth and nineteenth centuries marked the formation of the United States. During the eighteenth century, relations between Britain and its colony had grown worse and America declared itself independent in 1776. The declaration was drawn up by Thomas Jefferson. Britain recognised American independence seven years later. In 1789, George Washington was elected the first president. Relations between Britain and America remained poor. There were also wars between the Native American tribes and the settlers. Other European countries, such as France and Spain who had colonies in America, gradually gave up their hold but there was increasing division between the Northern and Southern states. Although the slave trade was abolished in 1808, slavery was still very much in existence. The Southern states depended on slave labour. Plantation and slave owners had grown wealthy from the slave trade and most Southerners wanted slavery retained. The abolitionists were in the North. Many abolition societies sprang up and were backed by the Church (although there were others who thought the matter should be left to individual states to decide). Bitterness grew and anti-slavery writings appeared. Matters came to a head when Abraham Lincoln, a strong abolitionist, became president. The American Civil War broke out in 1861. It lasted four years. The North (Unionists) won in 1865 and the Southern states were admitted back into the Union on condition that slavery was abolished.

© Folens (copiable page)

Mary Shelley: chronology

The following table allows you to see, at a glance, what important events were happening at the time Mary Shelley was writing. It includes her birth and her death and other important dates and events in her life.

Dates: births, deaths, marriage and selected writings

1797	Birth of Mary Shelley (née Godwin); death of mother, Mary Wollstonecraft
1814	Mary elopes with Percy Bysshe Shelley
1815	Birth and death of daughter
1816	Birth of William Shelley; death of Fanny Imlay; death of Harriet Shelley; marriage of Mary and Percy Bysshe Shelley
1817	Birth of Clara Shelley
1818	Original publication of *Frankenstein*; death of Clara
1819	Death of William; *Mathilda* (written)
1822	Death of Percy Bysshe Shelley
1823	*Valperga* (published)
1824	Death of Lord Byron
1826	*The Last Man* (published)
1830	*Perkin Warbeck* (published)
1831	Revised edition of *Frankenstein* (published)
1835	*Lodore* (published)
1837	*Falkner* (published)
1839	*Poetical Works* (of Percy Bysshe Shelley) (published)
1851	Death of Mary Shelley

Political and scientific events

1789	The French Revolution
1790	Luigi Galvani experiments with electricity and the movement of muscles
1804	Napoleon Bonaparte becomes Emperor of France
1805	Battle of Trafalgar
1807	Abolition of the slave trade in the British Empire
1811	Prince of Wales becomes Regent; Luddite riots
1814	Napoleon Bonaparte abdicates
1815	Battle of Waterloo; Corn Laws passed
1818	Experiments with blood transfusions
1819	Peterloo Massacre
1820	Death of George III
1825	Trades Unions legalised
1830	Death of George IV
1832	The Reform Act
1833	Abolition of slavery in the British Empire
1837	Death of William IV, Victoria acceeds
1842	Chartist riots
1846	Famine in Ireland
1851	The Great Exhibition

Edgar Allan Poe: chronology

The following table allows you to see at a glance what important events were happening at the time Edgar Allan Poe was writing. It includes his birth and his death and other important dates and events in his life.

Dates: births, deaths, marriage and selected writings	
1809	Birth of Edgar Allan Poe
1811	Death of mother, Elizabeth Arnold Hopkins Poe
1827	*Tamerlane and Other Poems* (published)
1829	*Al Aaraaf* (poems) (published)
1836	Marriage of Poe to Virginia Clemm
1838	'The Narrative of Arthur Gordon Pym' (published)
1839	'The Fall of the House of Usher' (published)
1841	'The Murders in the Rue Morgue' (published)
1842	Virginia becomes seriously ill, 'The Black Cat'; 'Eleonora' (published)
1843	'The Pit and The Pendulum' (published)
1844	'The Premature Burial' (published)
1847	Death of Virginia
1849	Death of Edgar Allan Poe

Historical events	
1776	American Declaration of Independence, Virginia is one of the original thirteen states
1783	Britain recognises the independence of the United States
1789	The French Revolution; American Constitution comes into operation; George Washington elected President
1800	The Northern states of America begin to emancipate slaves
1802	Louisiana purchased from France
1804	Bonaparte becomes Emperor of France
1807	Abolition of the slave trade in the British Empire
1808	Abolition of the slave trade in the United States
1814	Napoleon Bonaparte abdicates
1833	Abolition of slavery in the British Empire
1861–65	American Civil War
1865	Abolition of slavery in the United States

 © Folens (copiable page)

Summary of events

In the Preface of the 1818 edition of this novel, Percy Bysshe Shelley comments on the novel as though he were the author. In the 1831 edition, it is Mary Shelley's account. The following trace the main events of the novel.

Letters 1–4

Robert Walton opens the story through a series of letters to his sister about his journey to the North Pole. In Letter 4, he sees the monster briefly and also discovers Victor.

Chapters 1–10

Victor tells his story to Walton, who writes it down for his sister. He begins with an account of his happy but over-protective early life with his parents, Alphonse and Caroline Frankenstein. They discover Elizabeth Lavenza, a child living in poverty, and take her home. She becomes Victor's close companion. Henry Clerval, Victor's friend, is introduced and we learn about Victor's interest in science and his need to find the secret of life. Caroline dies. Her last request is that Victor and Elizabeth marry. Victor goes to University in Ingolstadt. He meets Professors M Krempe and M Waldman, disliking the former but admiring the latter. Victor becomes obsessed with creating a human and carries out experiments, becoming increasingly unstable, both physically and mentally. Finally, he creates life but is shocked by what he has made and has a breakdown. He is nursed back to health by Henry Clerval. He receives a letter from Elizabeth, continues his convalescence and tours the region with Clerval. Another letter arrives from home saying that William, Victor's younger brother, has been murdered. Victor returns home but, on the way, catches sight of the monster, who he believes is the murderer. On arrival, he discovers that Justine Moritz, a close family servant, has been accused. She stands trial and is executed. Victor feels that he is responsible. He seeks comfort in the stunning landscape of the Mont Blanc region. It is here that he meets the monster, who blames Victor for his wretchedness.

Chapters 11–17

The monster now takes over the story. Everyone he meets despises him. He describes observing the De Lacey family from a hiding place. They care for each other and he learns what love is. A young Arabian woman, Safie, arrives. She is taught English and, by watching from his hiding place, the monster also learns English and how to read. Among his clothes the monster finds Victor Frankenstein's notebook and discovers who has made him. He also discovers that the De Laceys have suffered too and he believes they will accept him. He approaches Mr De Lacey when the younger members are absent. The old man seems friendly, but he is blind. On their return, the younger members of the family are horrified and beat the monster. He is now embittered and seeks revenge. He burns down their home and determines to find his creator. As he approaches Geneva, he comes upon William. When he realises William is a Frankenstein he strangles him. The monster ends his story by asking Victor to make a female companion for him. Victor finally agrees.

Chapters 18–24

Marriage to Elizabeth is discussed but Victor decides to leave for Britain with Clerval. He begins creating a female in the Orkneys, alone. The monster appears at the window, Victor destroys the female and the monster delivers a threat. Victor sets out on a voyage to destroy his instruments in the sea, loses his way and is washed up in Ireland where he is arrested for murder. The victim turns out to be Clerval. Victor becomes delirious but is finally released and returns to Geneva where he marries Elizabeth. On his wedding night, the monster appears, as promised. He murders Elizabeth. Victor seeks revenge. After a visit to his family he begins his search for the monster, which takes him to the North Pole. There, he is saved by Robert Walton. Victor requests that if he dies Walton should kill the monster. The story is continued by Walton as a series of letters to his sister. Victor dies, repeating his request. The monster appears, saddened at his creator's death. He leaps from the cabin window on to the ice-raft ready to find the most northern point on the globe and die on his funeral pyre. He is lost in the darkness.

© Folens (copiable page)

Recording key events

FOCUS

- To use the timeline to show at a glance where key events occur.

- Select key events in the plot and mark them on the timeline. Include chapter and page references. You may also wish to note evidence of important themes or examples of style.

PRE-1914 CLASSICS: *Two Gothic Tales* © Folens (copiable page)

Victor Frankenstein

- To explore Victor Frankenstein's character.

● Make notes about Victor's character under the following headings. Refer to relevant quotations and include page numbers. The notes can be used to write essays and assignments and are useful for revision.

Age, appearance, position and social standing (note who Prometheus was and his relevance to Victor Frankenstein)

How others regard him (both initially and later on)

Character traits: strengths and weaknesses (what is his main weakness?)

Important actions taken

What he discovers about himself

The monster

- To explore the character of the monster.

● Make notes about the monster under the following headings. Refer to relevant quotations and include page numbers. The notes can be used to write essays and assignments and are useful for revision.

Origins, appearance, education (note that he has no name and the importance of this)

How others regard him

Character traits (how are these dominated by his circumstances?)

Important actions taken

What he learns about humanity and what he becomes

© Folens (copiable page)

Robert Walton

- To explore Robert Walton's character.

- Make notes about Robert Walton's character under the following headings. Refer to relevant quotations and include page numbers. The notes can be used to write essays and assignments and are useful for revision.

Age, appearance, social standing

How others regard him

Character traits: strengths and weaknesses

Important actions taken

How he develops, what he learns by the end of the novel

Elizabeth Frankenstein

FOCUS

- To explore the character of Elizabeth Frankenstein (née Lavenza).

- Make notes under the following headings. Refer to relevant quotations and include page numbers. The notes can be used to write essays and assignments and are useful for revision.

Age, appearance, social standing

How others regard her

Character traits: strengths and weaknesses (what does she represent?)

Important actions/non-actions

What happens to her

© Folens (copiable page)

Who's who? – other characters

FOCUS

- To revise the characteristics of other characters.

- Use the following information as a reference.

Justine Moritz
Treated badly by her mother and joins the Frankenstein family as a servant but becomes a member of the family. Falsely convicted and executed for the murder of William.

Safie
Wife of Felix De Lacey. Young, gentle, intelligent and the most single-minded and independent of the female characters. Has a Turkish father who is responsibile for the De Lacey's poverty. Safie travels to Germany to be with the De Laceys.

Henry Clerval
Young friend of Victor's, optimistic, romantic and enjoys heroic fiction.

M Waldman
Professor of chemistry at Ingolstadt. Middle-aged, short but dignified and mild mannered. Inspires Victor.

Also ...

Alphonse and Caroline Frankenstein
Affectionate over-protective parents of Victor. Alphonse is middle-aged, marries late and was previously a public figure. They have other children, Earnest and William, and raise Elizabeth. Caroline is presented as the ideal mother and also the ideal of feminine womanhood.

The De Laceys
Old De Lacey who is blind, his son Felix and daughter Agatha. Respectable French family but poor, having lost their money. It is from the De Laceys that the monster (who observes them in secret) learns about human interaction and the world. The De Laceys reject the monster when they set eyes on him.

M Krempe
Victor's professor of natural philosophy at Ingolstadt. Uncouth looking, short with a gruff voice. Does not approve of Victor studying alchemy.

Who says?

FOCUS

- To identify how well you know the characters and events in *Frankenstein*.

- Write down the details for each quotation in the space provided. Say on which page the quotation appears.

Said by _____

About _____

Volume _____

Chapter _____

1.

About five in the morning I discovered my lovely boy, whom the night before I had seen blooming and active in health …

2.

We perceived a low carriage, fixed on a sledge and drawn by dogs, pass on towards the north, at a distance of half a mile; a being which had the shape of a man, but apparently of gigantic stature …

3.

"And do you also believe that I am so very, very wicked? Do you also join with my enemies to crush me, to condemn me as a murderer?"

Said by _____

About _____

Volume _____   Chapter _____

Said by _____

About _____

Volume _____   Chapter _____

4.

My person was hideous and my stature gigantic. What did this mean? Who was I? What was I? Whence did I come?

Said by _____

About _____

Volume _____   Chapter _____

5.

These sublime and magnificent scenes afforded me the greatest consolation that I was capable of receiving. They elevated me from all littleness of feeling, and although they did not remove my grief, they subdued and tranquillized it.

6.

His limbs were in proportion, and I had selected his features as beautiful. Beautiful! Great God! His yellow skin scarcely covered the work of muscles and arteries beneath …

Said by _____

About _____

Volume _____   Chapter _____

Said by _____

About _____

Volume _____   Chapter _____

    PRE-1914 CLASSICS: *Two Gothic Tales*   © Folens (copiable page)

Beginning and end

FOCUS

● To understand and write about Robert Walton's letters.

Introduction

Robert Walton's letters to his sister, through which the story is told, provide a framework for the novel. Writing novels in this way is called **epistolary** ('epistle' means letter). It was very popular in the eighteenth century. However, Robert Walton's letters are important for other reasons, too.

1. Read these extracts from the letters at the beginning and the end of the novel.

a.

> St Petersburgh, Dec 11th 17—
>
> ... I feel a cold northern breeze play upon my cheeks, which braces my nerves, and fills me with delight. Do you understand this feeling? This breeze, which has travelled from the regions towards which I am advancing, gives me a foretaste of those icy climes. Inspirited by the wind of promise, my daydreams become more fervent and vivid. I try in vain to be persuaded that the pole is the seat of frost and desolation; it ever presents itself to my imagination as the region of beauty and delight.

(Letter 1)

b.

> September 12th
>
> It is past; I am returning to England. I have lost my hopes of utility and glory; – I have lost my friend. But I will endeavour to detail these bitter circumstances to you, my dear sister; and, while I am wafted towards England, and towards you, I will not despond.

(Chapter 24 Walton, *in continuation*)

2. What are the main differences in the tone (mood) of the extracts? Underline the words that best sum up the tone in each one.

3. Read both letters from which these extracts are taken and write 300 words explaining in what way they mirror the main story in the novel. In your conclusion, explain why you think a close friendship grew up between Robert Walton and Victor.

Telling the story 1

FOCUS

- To understand how the narrative voices relate to each other.

Introduction

There are several narrative voices in *Frankenstein* that are interrelated in a complex way. They are all in the first person but the overarching voice is that of Robert Walton. Here are the main features of the narrative voices. You can keep this page for reference.

- Robert Walton tells his and Victor Frankenstein's story through a series of letters and a manuscript.

- Victor Frankenstein tells his story to Robert Walton.

- The monster tells his story *usually* through Victor as he relates the story to Robert Walton.

- Other characters comment through Victor as he tells his story to Robert Walton.

- Some characters (such as De Lacey) speak through other characters (such as the monster) then through Victor, who is telling the story, to Robert Walton!

- After Victor's death, the voice of Robert Walton takes over completely and the monster speaks to him directly. However, we are reminded that Robert Walton has related *all the stories* in his letters or manuscript.

- From the reader's viewpoint, you can think of this complex series of voices as though they were Russian dolls. You open one doll and inside is another doll and then another and so on. However, in the chapters of this novel, the voices can shift. They are not always neatly arranged like Russian dolls!

PRE-1914 CLASSICS: *Two Gothic Tales* © Folens (copiable page)

Telling the story 2

FOCUS

- To identify the narrative voices and discuss the reliability of Victor's story.

- Use 'Telling the story 1' (provided by your teacher) to help you answer these questions.

1. Make notes saying who is speaking, about what and, where necessary, who is relating it. Find the chapter. The first has been done for you.

   a. "By the virtues that I once possessed, I demand this from you. Hear my tale; it is long and strange, and the temperature of this place is not fitting to your fine sensations …" (Chapter 10)

   Here the monster is speaking, demanding that Victor listen to his story.

   However, it is told by Victor. He is telling the story to Robert Walton, who has written it down.

   b. I have resolved every night, when I am not imperatively occupied by my duties, to record, as nearly as possible in his own words, what he has related during the day.
   (Letter 4)

   c. If I do [die], swear to me, Walton, that he shall not escape, that you will seek him and satisfy my vengeance in his death. (Chapter 24)

   d. Do not let this disturb you; do not answer tomorrow, or the next day, or even until you come, if it will give you pain. My uncle will send me news of your health … (Chapter 22)

   e. I had worked hard for nearly two years, for the sole purpose of infusing life into an inanimate body. (Chapter 5)

2. Write 150 words about why Victor's story could be unreliable. (Think about his personality, the way he presents the monster and what he wants Robert Walton to do.)

The language of the Gothic novel

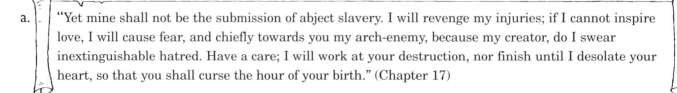

- To identify and make a critical assessment of the language used in the novel.

Introduction

The language used by Mary Shelley in *Frankenstein* is typical of the Gothic novel. It is melodramatic and highly descriptive. The quality varies. While some passages are well written and powerful, others are long-winded and tedious.

1. Read the following passages.

a. "Yet mine shall not be the submission of abject slavery. I will revenge my injuries; if I cannot inspire love, I will cause fear, and chiefly towards you my arch-enemy, because my creator, do I swear inextinguishable hatred. Have a care; I will work at your destruction, nor finish until I desolate your heart, so that you shall curse the hour of your birth." (Chapter 17)

b. The wind, which had fallen in the south, now rose with great violence in the west. The moon had reached her summit in the heavens and was beginning to descend; the clouds swept across it swifter than the flight of the vulture and dimmed her rays, while the lake reflected the scene of the busy heavens, rendered still busier by the restless waves that were beginning to rise. Suddenly a heavy storm of rain descended. (Chapter 23)

2. Which do you think is the better piece of writing? Annotate the text, underlining phrases, images and punctuation that you feel add to the expression in one colour and those you think detract from it, in another.

Consider these questions.

- Are there too many repetitions?

- Are powerful words used?

- Is the punctuation used to vary the pace?

- Are the sentences too long?

- Is it emotionally moving or tedious?

- Are there interesting allusions (references) to other parts of the novel?

- Are some parts better than others within each passage?

- Is it cumbersome to read aloud or does it flow?

But remember, you should not try to compare the passages with the language of a modern novel. Try to judge them within the terms of the Gothic.

Making connections

FOCUS

- To understand what 'allusion' is and how it is used in the novel and to make connections between *Frankenstein* and modern-day allusions.

Introduction

From time to time, Mary Shelley **alludes** (makes reference) to other literature in the novel. These allusions would be known to the readers of the day and some are still recognisable to us.

1. The following is quoted in Chapter 5. What connection does it have to *Frankenstein*?

   Like one, that on a lonesome road
   Doth walk in fear and dread,
   And having once turned round walks on,
   And turns no more his head;
   Because he knows, a frightful fiend
   Doth close behind him tread.

   from *The Rime of the Ancient Mariner* by Samuel Taylor Coleridge

2. Draw up a list of modern-day allusions to *Frankenstein*. Consider what is depicted in literature, film, television, advertisements and any other media you can think of. Use the illustrations below to help you.

3. Write a comment next to each one, saying what its connection is to *Frankenstein*.

   For example:
   The 'Addams Family' is a comic interpretation of the Gothic, with a depiction of the monster.

   Remember, your choices do not have to be Gothic, they can allude to themes and other aspects of the novel.

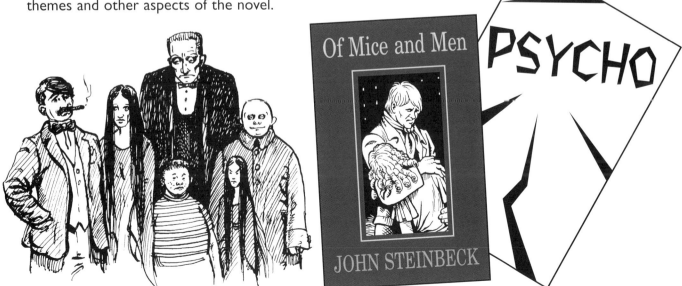

The modern Prometheus

FOCUS

- To understand what the full title of the novel alludes to and its significance.

Introduction

Prometheus was a Titan in Greek mythology. 'Titan' is associated with great strength and power and the name means 'forethought'. In one story, Prometheus tricked Zeus, stole fire (often seen as one of the 'makers of life') and was cast out to the icy Mount Caucasus, to what was regarded as the most easterly point of the world. Each day, a vulture fed on his liver, but it was renewed at night. Percy Bysshe Shelley also wrote a dramatic poem called *Prometheus Unbound* (1820).

1. Look carefully at the illustrations.

a.
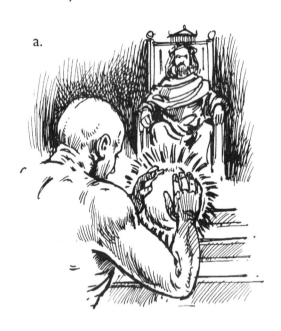

b.
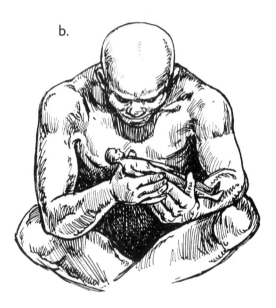

c.

2. Make notes about any links between Prometheus and the *Frankenstein* story.

© Folens (copiable page)

On screen

FOCUS

- To compare aspects of the film *Mary Shelley's Frankenstein* with the book.

Introduction

There have been many film versions of *Frankenstein*. Some bear little resemblance to the novel, while others follow it more closely. In a screen adaptation, there are inevitably changes. Kenneth Branagh's film, *Mary Shelley's Frankenstein* is one of the most recent adaptations.

1. Consider these questions when studying the film and make brief notes.

   a. **Characters**

   How does the depiction of these characters differ in the film and the book?

   Elizabeth   Robert Walton   M Krempe   M Waldman

   Think about:
   - their actions and behaviour
   - the importance of the character in the film compared with the novel
   - what point Kenneth Branagh was making (e.g. Elizabeth is more assertive in the film).

   b. **Plot**

   There are several changes to the plot in the film. What happens to these characters?

   Justine Moritz   Elizabeth   Henry Clerval   Alphonse Frankenstein

   Think about:
   - how each differs from the book
   - the purpose of these changes (e.g. consider Justine's lynching as well as other aspects about her).

   What other changes in the plot did you notice? What are the reasons for them?

   c. **The monster**

   Do you think the monster is more monstrous in the film or the book? Say why.

   At the end of the film the monster refers to Victor as his father. Is this in keeping with the book or not? Note why/why not.

   d. These words, said by Walton in the film, do not appear in the book: "For in much wisdom is much grief, and he that increaseth knowledge increaseth sorrow."

   Say whether Mary Shelley would have approved of these words being used, and why.

   e. Do you think the dialogue, setting, costumes, camera and general direction suit the Gothic novel sufficiently? Should they?

2. Do you think Kenneth Branagh's film is Mary Shelley's or Kenneth Branagh's? Is it in the spirit of the book or does it differ in important ways?

The monster: what am I?

FOCUS

- To explain what themes you think the monster is linked to.

Introduction

The monster can be viewed as a character, a symbol (what it represents) and a theme (an idea running through the novel). It has no identity, no name and belongs nowhere. But it does have consciousness and is linked to humanity through its creator, Victor Frankenstein. What do you think it is? Can it be several things? Do you think it is appropriate even to call it a 'monster'?

1. Read the following statements. Put those you agree with in order of importance, as they relate to the novel.

The monster is:

- a victim of society

- an outsider

- an aspect of Victor Frankenstein's imagination

- the darker side of Victor Frankenstein

- a demon, devil or the embodiment of evil

- a split personality

- a scientific exploration by Mary Shelley

- an innocent

- untamed strength

- a human without understanding or morals

- an unloved creature

- a non-human

- good turned into bad.

2. Choose the three most important statements. Write three paragraphs (about 300 words) explaining why you have chosen them. You will need to refer to the novel to support what you say.

 © Folens (copiable page)

Playing God

FOCUS

- To consider the relevance of *Frankenstein* in the modern age.

Introduction

One of the reasons why *Frankenstein* has remained so popular is that it lends itself easily to issues of the modern age; issues that focus on scientific developments relevant to us.

1. Identify the following symbolic representations of scientific developments.

2. Is the example relevant to *Frankenstein*? If so how/how not?

   Discuss this question and then write notes underneath each image.

3. Now discuss these additional points with a partner:

   a. Do you think Victor's treatment of the monster is as bad as creating life in any of the ways above?

   b. Do you think the society's treatment of the monster is as bad?

   c. What are your own views about modern scientific developments in genetics?

The Doppelgänger

FOCUS

- To identify how the monster and Victor Frankenstein can be viewed as different sides of the same person.

Introduction

Doppelgänger is a German word first used in the nineteenth century. It means 'double' (literally 'double-goer'). It is a ghost or reflection of the person.

1. Read the quotations below. They are all spoken by Victor. What do they reveal?

   Consider:
   - what is unleashed in Victor by his need to create human life
   - what consumes him when he has created the monster.

2. Underline key words and write down what they reveal about Victor's personality.

   a. I saw how the fine form of man was degraded and wasted; I beheld the corruption of death succeed to the blooming cheek of life … (Chapter 4)

   b. Who shall conceive the horrors of my secret toil as I dabbled among the unhallowed damps of the grave or tortured the living animal to animate the lifeless clay? … I seemed to have lost all soul or sensation but for this one pursuit. (Chapter 4)

   c. It was to be decided whether the result of my curiosity and lawless devices would cause the death of two of my fellow beings … (Chapter 8)

   d. A fiend has snatched from me every hope of future happiness; no creature had ever been so miserable as I was … Mine has been a tale of horrors … (Chapter 23)

   e. Again do I vow vengeance; again do I devote thee, miserable fiend, to torture and death. (Chapter 24)

3. Write a paragraph describing what side of Victor's personality the monster represents. Do you think we all have these tendencies in us? Give reasons for your answer.

 © Folens (copiable page)

Victims and crimes

FOCUS

- To understand and identify the different ways in which 'the victim' and injustice operate in the novel.

Introduction

In *Frankenstein*, both these themes are common. Characters can be victims or commit injustices, or fit into both categories. They may sometimes be victims of themselves, by pursuing a particular course of action. There are also characters who are victims of fate or who suffer at the hands of institutions.

1. Consider the following and tick which boxes apply to each. Then makes notes to say why. (Think carefully, a character may suffer from or commit more than one injustice.)

	Victim	Commits an injustice	Why
William Frankenstein			
Felix De Lacey			
Victor Frankenstein			
Elizabeth Lavenza			
The monster			
The law (in the case of Justine Moritz)			
Safie's father			
Caroline Frankenstein			
De Lacey			

2. Choose two of the above and find quotations to support what you say.

3. Can you think of any character that is neither a victim nor one who commits an injustice? Say why.

Outcast

FOCUS

● To identify different examples of alienation in the novel.

Introduction

Alienation means being isolated from a social group, a society or an activity. It is a common theme in modern novels and other media. Alienated characters can be outcasts or may be alienated from themselves, so that they see no purpose in the life they lead. Other characters may be estranged in some way, and scenes and settings can also suggest alienation.

The most obvious example of alienation in *Frankenstein* is the monster, who belongs nowhere, but there are other examples, too.

1. Look at the following. Write notes explaining how each one of these is in some way alienated – or outside the 'normal' world. In some cases there may be more than one way.

Safie

Victor Frankenstein

Robert Walton

Justine Moritz

Landscape of ice and snow

2. De Lacey may also be considered as an alienated character. Do you agree?

3. What examples of science-fiction stories, novels, films or television plays/series can you think of that are linked to alienation? Draw up a list. Choose one that has other links to *Frankenstein* and say how. Write about 300 words.

 © Folens (copiable page)

Other themes

FOCUS

● To explore other themes in the novel and their significance.

Introduction
There are many themes in *Frankenstein* and they are often interrelated.

1. The following illustrations represent death, chaos and madness, beauty versus ugliness, family life, and knowledge. Decide which is which and write down two examples in the novel for each theme. Note in which chapter they occur. Add any other important information. (e.g. under 'family life' you could add: 'mothers are either non-existent, die or are bad mothers.')

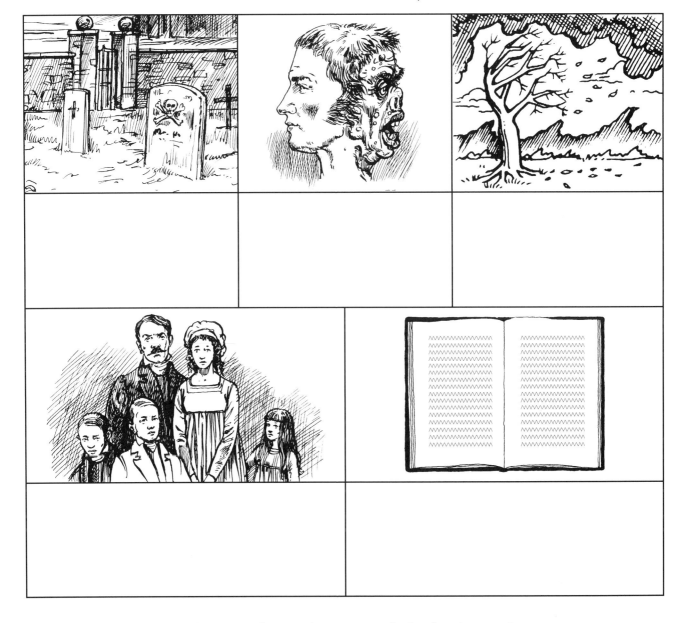

2. Make a note of any other themes and examples you can think of in the novel.

Summary of events

The narrator (no name is given) introduces the story as both a confession and 'a homely narrative' from the condemned cell.

His infancy and boyhood are described. He was, we are told, mild-mannered, tender of heart and a lover of animals.

His wife is of the same temperament, also a lover of animals, but has a tendency to superstition.

Their favourite pet is a black cat called Pluto.

For several years, the narrator, his wife and their pets live together happily, but gradually the narrator becomes addicted to alcohol – 'the Fiend Intemperance'. He undergoes an extreme change of personality, neglecting his wife and pets alike, except for Pluto.

As the disease grows, so does the abuse of his wife and the animals, until Pluto also becomes a target.

One night, the drunk narrator grasps the cat and, with a penknife, cuts out one of its eyes. He feels something like remorse the next day. The cat avoids him in terror.

Soon after, the narrator, becoming increasingly violent, slips a noose around the animal's neck and hangs it from a tree. That night the house catches fire. The narrator and his wife manage to escape but the flames take all his worldly wealth.

The narrator visits the ruins of the house the next day, where a wall in the middle of the house remains standing. A crowd has gathered to look at an embossed picture on the wall. It is of a gigantic cat with a rope around its neck. The narrator convinces himself that someone must have thrown Pluto in through the bedroom window to wake him when the fire started and the cat has become compressed between this and a tumbling wall.

The narrator cannot get rid of the image from his mind and searches for another cat. He finds an identical one, with the exception that it has a white patch of fur. He takes it home.

Subsequently, he takes a dislike to the creature. This grows into hatred, particularly because it has one eye like Pluto and because it follows him around. In addition, the white patch has grown into the shape of the 'gallows'.

The narrator overcomes all sense of guilt and fear of the cat. He grows increasingly violent and one day in the cellar, attempts to aim a blow at the animal, using an axe. His wife tries to prevent him. He aims another blow, this time at his wife and kills her.

He coolly conceals the body by successfully walling it up in the cellar. He then searches for the cat, which, to his relief, is nowhere to be found. The narrator sleeps peacefully that night.

Four days later, a group of policemen arrive but nothing is discovered. The narrator, over-confident, demonstrates how well the house is built. He raps on the wall where the body is concealed. An unearthly noise grows into a howl. The policemen tear down the wall and find not only the decaying body but, on its head, the black cat, 'with red mouth extended and solitary eye of fire'.

Recording key events

FOCUS

- To use the timeline to show at a glance where key events occur.

- Select key events in the story and mark them on the timeline. Include page references. You may also wish to note evidence of important themes or aspects of style (e.g. the reliability of the narrative voice).

The narrator

- To explore the narrator's character.

- Make notes about the narrator under the following headings. Refer to relevant quotations and include page numbers. The notes can be used to write essays and assignments and are useful for revision.

Important information we *don't* know about him (e.g. his name)

Important actions taken

Character traits at the beginning of the story

What the narrator learns/confirms about himself

Character traits by the end of the story

Where the narrator is when he tells the story

Pluto

FOCUS

● To explore Pluto's character.

● Make notes about the cat under the following headings. Refer to relevant quotations and include page numbers. The notes can be used to write essays and assignments and are useful for revision.

Significance of name (note who gave it the name)

How the cat changes and why

What we are told at the beginning of the story about the cat's nature

The narrator's view of the cat (what is believable/not believable)

What the cat symbolises

The narrator's wife

● To explore the wife's character.

● Make notes about the narrator's wife under the following headings. Refer to relevant quotations and include page numbers. The notes can be used to write essays and assignments and are useful for revision.

Important information we *don't* know about her

Actions (if any)

Character traits

Actions against her

What she symbolises

               © Folens (copiable page)

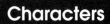

Key quotations

FOCUS

- To identify key quotations in the story and their significance.

1. Complete the table by identifying where in the story the following quotations occur, what they mean and why they are important.

2. Add other important quotations and details and keep the table for reference.

Quotation	Where it occurs in the story	Meaning/importance
a. Yet, mad am I not – and very surely do I not dream.		
b. From my infancy I was noted for the docility and humanity of my disposition.		
c. … my wife … made frequent allusion to the ancient popular notion, which regarded all black cats as witches in disguise.		

The narrative voice

FOCUS

- To understand and write about the features of the narrative voice in 'The Black Cat'.

1. Tick the boxes next to the statements you agree with.

The narrative voice

a. is written in the

- first person ☐

- third person ☐

b. is a character

- in the story ☐

- outside the story ☐

c. tells the story

- from a single point of view ☐

- from several characters' points of view ☐

d. • always exaggerates ☐

- sometimes exaggerates ☐

- never exaggerates ☐

e. • believes the story ☐

- does not believe the story ☐

f. expects the reader

- to believe the story ☐

- not to believe the story. ☐

2. Write 150 words saying whether or not we should trust what the narrative voice tells us. Give reasons for your answer.

Symbols

FOCUS

● To identify and explain some of the symbols in 'The Black Cat'.

Introduction

Symbols can be used to represent the ideas and themes running through a story. For example, a withering rose could be a symbol of old age. The most important symbol in 'The Black Cat' is the cat itself. However, there are other symbols in the story that are linked to it.

1. Write brief notes underneath to say what you think each symbol represents. A symbol may represent more than one thing and several symbols can represent the same thing. An example has been done for you.

A single eye	**The name of the cat**	**A noose**
The single eye represents evil. It is linked to the cutting out of the black cat's eye and also the cat's 'eye of fire' when the wall is dismantled.		
A Gothic house on fire	**Gallows**	**A gloomy cellar**

Poe's use of language

FOCUS
- To understand difficult passages in 'The Black Cat'.

Introduction
Edgar Allan Poe's use of language is similar to the language of other Gothic tales. It is intense language used to create fear and horror. However, Poe also uses it to present ideas.

1. Read this passage.

And then came, as if to my final and irrevocable overthrow, the spirit of PERVERSENESS. Of this spirit philosophy takes no account. Yet I am not more sure that my soul lives, than I am that perverseness is one of the primitive impulses of the human heart – one of the indivisible primary faculties, or sentiments, which give direction to the character of Man. Who has not, a hundred times, found himself committing a vile or a stupid action, for no other reason than because he knows he should *not*? Have we not a perpetual inclination, in the teeth of our best judgement, to violate that which is *Law*, merely because we understand it to be such? This spirit of perverseness, I say, came to my final overthrow. It was this unfathomable longing of the soul *to vex itself* – to offer violence to its own nature – to do wrong for the wrong's sake only …

Use the following approach to work out its meaning.

2. Write down a sentence summing up what you think the passage is about.

_____

_____

3. Now underline all, or the most difficult of the words you do not know and write them in a table as shown below. (Include the word 'perverseness'.)

Words	My guess	Definition

4. Referring to the passage, write down in the next column, 'My guess', what you think the word could mean.

5. Check the meaning of the words in a dictionary and write them under 'Definition' if it is different from your guess.

6. Rewrite your sentence from question 2 and turn it into a short paragraph explaining the passage more fully. Try to comment on the complex parts of the passage.

Climaxes

FOCUS

- To identify the main climax and other climaxes in the story.

Introduction

'The Black Cat' has one main **climax** (exciting and most important point) and several minor ones.

1. Identify each incident in the story below and write comments explaining what is happening. Tick the type of climax you think it is.

   a. 'One morning, in cold blood, I slipped a noose about its neck and ...'

   _____

   ☐ main ☐ minor

   b.

   _____

   _____

   ☐ main ☐ minor

   c. 'I approached and saw, as if graven in *bas-relief* upon the white surface, the figure of a gigantic *cat*. The impression was given with an accuracy truly marvellous. There was ...'

   _____

   ☐ main ☐ minor

   d.

   _____

   _____

   ☐ main ☐ minor

   e. 'I took from my waistcoat pocket a penknife, opened it, grasped the poor beast ...'

   _____

   ☐ major ☐ minor

2. Now select the main climax. Write a paragraph explaining your choice.

Features of the Gothic tale

FOCUS

- To understand some of the features of the Gothic tale and to identify examples in 'The Black Cat'.

Introduction

'The Black Cat' contains typical features of the Gothic tale and shares similarities with other short stories by Edgar Allan Poe.

1. Read the list below and record examples from 'The Black Cat' along with any other important points you know about. The first has been done for you.

   a. The characters and places have no name.

   Only the cat Pluto has a name. (Pluto was the god of the underworld in Greek mythology.)

   We are not told the name of the place or setting where the story takes place.

   b. There is a ghostly atmosphere.

   c. There are secret doors, long corridors and strange rooms.

   d. Characters may return from the dead.

   e. Characters may have a 'sixth sense' or psychic powers.

2. From what you have learned about the Gothic tale. (Think of other stories, such as *Dracula*, to help you). Add another feature you think is typical and find an example in 'The Black Cat'.

Madness

FOCUS

- To discuss and write about the theme of madness and decide whether or not the opening paragraph of the story is **ironic**.

1. Find the opening paragraph of the story and read it. Now read the following.

The narrator opens the story by telling us that he does not expect the reader to believe him – that he would be 'mad' to think we could believe him. He assures us, however, that he is not mad and he presents to us, clearly and rationally, a series of events that describe his descent into madness.

2. Do you think he's mad?

3. Find:

   a. two examples in the story where the main character loses control

   b. two examples where he remains in control while carrying out dreadful acts.

4. Referring to your examples, discuss with a partner:

   a. how the narrator feels about his actions (does this change?)

   b. whether or not he is mad, evil or behaves as he does for other reasons

   c. whether or not the opening passage is ironic (saying or showing the opposite of what is intended).

5. What do you think Edgar Allan Poe wants us to think about his character's state of mind? Write 300 words referring to the work you have already done.

The divided personality

FOCUS

● To consider the two sides of the narrator's personality.

Introduction
At the beginning of the story, the narrator's personality is described. It is in sharp contrast to the way in which he acts later.

1. Read the following description. Underline in blue the words and phrases that describe the narrator's personality. Use a dictionary to check words you do not know.

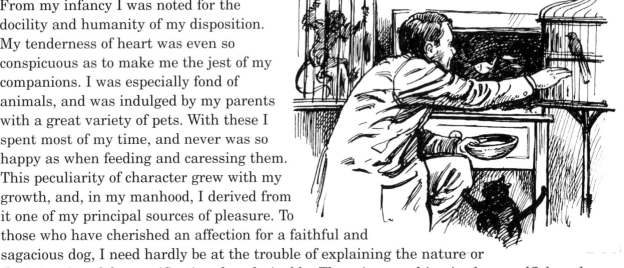

From my infancy I was noted for the docility and humanity of my disposition. My tenderness of heart was even so conspicuous as to make me the jest of my companions. I was especially fond of animals, and was indulged by my parents with a great variety of pets. With these I spent most of my time, and never was so happy as when feeding and caressing them. This peculiarity of character grew with my growth, and, in my manhood, I derived from it one of my principal sources of pleasure. To those who have cherished an affection for a faithful and sagacious dog, I need hardly be at the trouble of explaining the nature or the intensity of the gratification thus derivable. There is something in the unselfish and self-sacrificing love of a brute, which goes directly to the heart of him who has had frequent occasion to test the paltry friendship and gossamer fidelity of mere *Man*.

2. Write down three examples of actions taken later that are the opposite of the personality described.

    a. _____

    _____

    b. _____

    _____

    c. _____

    _____

3. Write 450 words to say how the narrator's character begins to deteriorate and what it is like by the end. Refer to the story to support what you say.

PRE-1914 CLASSICS: *Two Gothic Tales*   © Folens (copiable page)

The supernatural

FOCUS

- To identify what the second black cat represents.

Introduction

In Poe's stories, the supernatural can often represent the psychological breakdown of a character. By the end of 'The Black Cat', the narrator refers to the second cat as 'the hideous beast whose craft had seduced me into murder'. So, the narrator does not seem able to take responsibility for his actions.

1. What else do you think the second black cat in the story represents? Tick those statements you agree with. (You may tick as many as you like.)

a demon ☐

the reincarnation of Pluto ☐

the narrator's fear ☐

the narrator's sense of guilt ☐

an ordinary cat ☐

punishment or revenge ☐

a delusion (i.e. there is not really a second cat) ☐

death ☐

a death wish on the part of the narrator ☐

the desire to commit evil acts. ☐

2. Now write 300 words saying what you think the second black cat most represents and why. Refer to other symbols in the story if you wish.

PRE-1914 CLASSICS: *Two Gothic Tales*

Stepping over the boundaries

FOCUS

- To identify and write about why the narrator commits criminal acts in 'The Black Cat'.

Introduction

During the story the narrator is torn between the good and bad sides of his personality until, at the end, he feels no guilt for committing crimes. Stepping over the boundaries or 'transgressing' (which literally means 'stepping across') is common in the Gothic tale, which is concerned with the inner workings of the mind.

1. Complete the examples given below, in which someone commits serious crimes. Each crime should be more serious than the last. List reasons why the person commits them. (Think of at least four reasons for each one. Some reasons may be the same, but your list should vary as well.)

Crime	Possible reasons
a. Stealing cars	makes him or her feel powerful the thrill he or she is out of control poverty
b.	
c.	

2. What is the most important reason the narrator would give for committing crimes? Do you think there is any truth in this? Write 300 words to explain your answer.

'Lady Lazarus' and 'The Black Cat'

Introduction

Sylvia Plath was born in America in 1932. She was a poet and novelist who lived in Britain with her husband, the late Poet Laureate, Ted Hughes. Her first book of poems *The Colossus* was published in 1960, her novel *The Bell Jar* in 1963 and the volume from which this poem comes, *Ariel*, in 1965, after her death. Many of her poems are concerned with harrowing emotions, although her writing is very tightly structured. She committed suicide in 1963.

Essay title

Compare the themes and language of 'Lady Lazarus' by Sylvia Plath and 'The Black Cat' by Edgar Allan Poe.

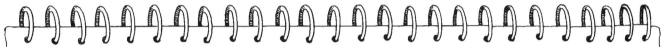

Planning

Stage 1: You should find out who Lazarus was, if you do not already know. In addition, carry out some research on the Holocaust and its significance in World War II. Later you can assess its relevance to the poem.

Stage 2: Read the poem through several times and identify the main themes in the poem (such as 'death'). What other themes are there?

Ask yourself questions. (For example: what does 'it' refer to in line 1 – 'I have done it again'? How might this relate to 'The Black Cat'?)

Next, note down the best thematic links (no more than three) that you can find between the poem and the story.

Stage 3: Now look more closely at the language of 'Lady Lazarus'. Underline the many words and phrases that relate to 'The Black Cat'. Think about the tone (mood) and images such as similes and metaphors. For example: *the tone is grotesque, macabre; a simile is 'And like the cat I have nine times to die' (line 21); a metaphor is 'The grate cave ate' (line 17).*

How do these features relate to 'The Black Cat'? How does Lazarus relate to it?

Stage 4: Find specific examples in the story that link to the poem. (You will need to consider the cat in its different guises.)

Stage 5: In what way is the poem different from 'The Black Cat'? For example, consider how the language differs. Although the tone of the poem is grotesque and horrifying, it is not melodramatic (as the language used in the story is). What else do you notice?

● Write your assignment but remember to draw on the research you have done into the historical or cultural period of both works, commenting on the way these influence the writers.

'Lady Lazarus'
by Sylvia Plath

I have done it again.
One year in every ten
I manage it—

A sort of walking miracle, my skin
Bright as a Nazi lampshade,
My right foot

A paperweight,
My face a featureless, fine
Jew linen.

Peel of the napkin
O my enemy.
Do I terrify?—

The nose, the eye pits, the full set of teeth?
The sour breath
Will vanish in a day.

Soon, soon the flesh
The grave cave ate will be
At home on me

And I am a smiling woman.
I am only thirty.
And like the cat I have nine times to die.

This is Number Three.
What a trash
To annihilate each decade.

What a million filaments.
The peanut-crunching crowd
Shoves in to see

Them unwrap me hand and foot—
The big strip tease.
Gentleman, ladies

These are my hands
My knees.
I may be skin and bone,

Nevertheless, I am the same, identical woman.
The first time it happened I was ten.
It was an accident.

The second time I meant
To last it out and not come back at all.
I rocked shut

© Folens (copiable page)

As a seashell.
They had to call and call
And pick the worms off me like sticky pearls.

Dying
Is an art, like everything else.
I do it exceptionally well.

I do it so it feels like hell.
I do it so it feels real.
I guess you could say I've a call.

It's easy enough to do it in a cell.
It's easy enough to do it and stay put.
It's the theatrical

Comeback in broad day
To the same place, the same face, the same brute
Amused shout:

'A miracle!'
That knocks me out.
There is a charge

For the eyeing of my scars, there is charge
For the hearing of my heart—
It really goes.

And there is a charge, a very large charge
For a word or a touch
Or a bit of blood

Or a piece of my hair or my clothes.
So, so, Herr Doktor.
So, Herr Enemy.

I am your opus,
I am your valuable,
The pure gold baby

That melts to a shriek.
I turn and burn.
Do not think I underestimate your great concern.

Ash, ash—
You poke and stir.
Flesh, bone, there is nothing there—

A cake of soap,
A wedding ring,
A gold filling.

Herr God, Herr Lucifer
Beware
Beware.

Out of the ash
I rise with my red hair
And I eat men like air.

Lennie

Introduction
John Steinbeck (1902–68) was an American novelist who lived through the Great Depression of the 1930s. *Of Mice and Men* (1937) is concerned with migrant agricultural labourers who crossed California in search of work.

 Essay title

Write a comparison between Lennie in *Of Mice and Men* by John Steinbeck and the monster in *Frankenstein* by Mary Shelley.

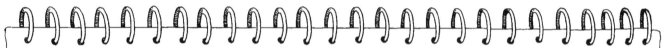

Planning

Stage 1: You need to find out more about the economic Depression of the 1930s, particularly among agricultural workers, and the unemployment and the alienation this caused. (Ensure you understand what 'alienation' is.) You should also find out about John Steinbeck's concerns in other novels such as *The Grapes of Wrath* (1939).

Stage 2: Consider the character of Lennie, his physical appearance, attitudes, what he does and what happens to him. Consider also his relationship with George; in what sense are both 'alienated' and why? (Note George's speech on 'loneliness' in the first chapter.)

Stage 3: Similarities
How is Lennie similar to the monster in *Frankenstein*? There are several parallels to be drawn. For example, in what way is Lennie regarded as a 'monster' in the story? What important incidents occur that govern other characters' attitudes to him? What themes in the novel, apart from alienation, connect with those in *Frankenstein*, particularly with regard to the monster?

Stage 4: Differences
How does Lennie differ from the monster? (Think about Lennie's intentions compared with the monster's.) How does the monster change? In what sense is he more aware than Lennie? How does George's attitude to Lennie differ from Victor Frankenstein's attitude to the monster?

What other differences can you think of?

You could draw up a table for Stages 3 and 4 and list the similarities and differences.

Stage 5: You should also look at the different ways the authors regard the characters. In what sense is John Steinbeck sympathetic to his character and Mary Shelley not? What is the popular view today of the monster in *Frankenstein*? What does this tell you about the different historical periods in which the stories are set and the changing attitudes?

● Draw all your work together, including useful references and quotations, to write your assignment.

   © Folens (copiable page)

The outsider

Introduction
Robert Swindells has written many stories for children. The main characters often find themselves under threat and his stories focus on their survival. He deals with topical issues such as homelessness (*Stone Cold* 1994), historical ones such as the holocaust (*Brother In The Land* 1984) and some, like *Daz 4 Zoe* (1990), are set in the future.

 Essay title

Look at the treatment of the outsider in *Daz 4 Zoe* by Robert Swindells and in *Frankenstein* by Mary Shelley.

Planning

Stage 1: One of the main themes of *Daz 4 Zoe* is alienation (or isolation from a social group, or society). Write about the following.

Who are the outsiders in *Daz 4 Zoe*? Consider the positions of the characters at the beginning of the novel and what happens to them. Who are they alienated from and why? Consider also the bleak inner city descriptions and the fear and isolation of the Subbies. What else in the novel implies alienation? Refer to specific examples.

Stage 2: Now make notes on the outsider in *Frankenstein*.

Remember, the monster is not the only one who becomes alienated from society. Who else is or becomes an outsider? (Consider minor characters such as Justine and old Mr De Lacey as well as major ones.) How else does the novel depict alienation?

Stage 3: In what way does the treatment of the outsider differ in each novel? What are the outcomes for the characters? Are the endings positive or not? Where are our sympathies meant to lie? What features in each novel tell us when the novels were written and set?

Stage 4: *Daz 4 Zoe* is a science-fiction novel. *Frankenstein* was written before the term 'science fiction' was coined. Yet the two types of novels have connections. What would you say these were? When you write your assignment, conclude with comments that address these points. In addition, show how the treatment of the outsider is affected by the concerns of the society in which the stories are set.

You could extend your assignment and include other novels which also discuss the outsider, such as *Of Mice and Men*. Look at the differences and similarities between them and the historical periods in which they were written.

The act of creation

Introduction

Vernon Scannell is well known for his range of subjects and his technical skill. His writing explores many areas of everyday life in the twentieth century. He is also a radio and television broadcaster. His concern with the creative process – how and what we create – is one that is addressed by many poets, writers and artists.

Essay title

To draw parallels between the poem 'Makers and Creatures' by Vernon Scannell and *Frankenstein* by Mary Shelley, taking account of the periods in which they were written.

Planning

Stage 1: Read 'Makers and Creatures', ensuring you understand what it is about. Then write a short introductory paragraph outlining the main similarity between the poem and *Frankenstein* and the usefulness of comparing the two works.

Stage 2: Now take a more detailed look at the poem. Underline any useful phrases that have links with the main theme in *Frankenstein* (i.e. the act of creation). There are many examples (e.g. lines 8–9 '… fail/At first to see that it's your own.').

Stage 3: When you feel you know the poem well, consider the following questions:
● What are the poet's responses to his creation?
● What does he feel God's responses are?
● What is Victor Frankenstein's response?

Stage 4: To help you think clearly, you could draw up a table noting answers to the questions in **Stage 3**. You might take a line from the poem to help you.
'And how do all the/Makers feel to see their creatures live?' (lines 17–18)

The poet's views	The poet's view of what God feels	Victor Frankenstein's view

● Now write up your notes, referring to the poem and the novel for evidence.

Stage 5: Finally, you could conclude by:
● drawing out what the poet feels is God's view when he created a human (remembering that this is expressed in modern terms) and comparing this with Victor Frankenstein's view

● considering whether or not Mary Shelley's view about 'playing God' in her novel is still relevant to us today and, if so, how.

PRE-1914 CLASSICS: *Two Gothic Tales*
© Folens (copiable page)

'Makers and Creatures'
by Vernon Scannell

It is a curious experience
And one you're bound to know, though probably
In other realms than that of literature,
Though I speak of poems now, assuming
That you are interested, otherwise,
Of course, you wouldn't be reading this;
It is strange to come across a poem
In a magazine or book and fail
At first to see that it's your own.
Sometimes you think, grateful and surprised,
'That's really not too bad', or gloomily:
'Many have done as well and far, far better'.
Or, in despair, 'My God, that's terrible.
What was I thinking of to publish it!'
And then you start to wonder how the great
Poets felt, seeing, surprised, their poems
As strangers, beautiful. And how do all the
Makers feel to see their creatures live?
The carpenter, the architect, the man who
Crochets intricate embroideries
Of steel across the sky. And how does God
Feel, looking at his poems, his creatures?
The swelling inhalation of plump hills,
Plumage of poplars on the pale horizon,
Fishleap flashing in pools cool as silver,
Great horses haunched with glossy muscles,
Birds who spray their song like apple juice,
And the soft shock of snow. He must feel good
Surprised again by these. But what happens
When he takes a look at man? Does he say,
'That's really not too bad', or does he, as I fear,
Wince once and mutter to himself:
'What was I thinking of publishing that one?'

© Folens (copiable page)

'The Ratcatcher' and 'The Black Cat'

FOCUS

- To explore the similarities and differences in the way horror is created in 'The Ratcatcher' by Roald Dahl and 'The Black Cat' by Edgar Allan Poe.

- It is best to read the whole of 'The Ratcatcher' before considering the suggestions below. Note any other ideas you have that may be useful as the focus for an assignment.

Roald Dahl (1916–1990) is well known not only for his children's stories but also his adult fiction, which is often disturbing, hovering as it does between reality and fantasy. His settings are commonplace, even mundane, but the events that occur and the characters he creates are sinister.

Stage 1: After you have read 'The Ratcatcher', refer to the extract that comes from the opening page of the story. Consider these questions:
- What is the setting like?
- How is the ratcatcher depicted in appearance and character? (Look at the description carefully.) Underline the text for useful words and phrases.
- What is the conversation like between the ratcatcher and Claud? What kind of language is used?

Stage 2: Use your knowledge of 'The Black Cat' and what you know of the period and focus on the similarities and differences between the stories. (For example, how do the two authors use animals in creating 'horror'? How do the settings differ? What does this tell us about when the stories were written?)

Stage 3: Draw up two tables, one in which you compare the similarities and one in which you compare the differences between 'The Ratcatcher' and 'The Black Cat'. An example is given below.

'The Ratcatcher' and 'The Black Cat'

Similarities	Evidence: 'The Ratcatcher'	Evidence: 'The Black Cat'
use of surprise to create horror	when the ratcatcher devours the rat	when the narrator cuts out the cat's eye

Differences	Evidence: 'The Ratcatcher'	Evidence: 'The Black Cat'
setting	ordinary, everyday	description vague, mysterious

Note some useful quotations to support what you say.

Stage 4: You should try to read more stories in the collection from which 'The Ratcatcher' comes (*Claud's Dog*) and you need to discuss in your assignment the different historical and cultural periods in which the stories are set. In the work you have already done, you will have considered this and you should pull the main points together in your conclusion.

'The Ratcatcher'
from *Claud's Dog* by Roald Dahl

In the afternoon the ratcatcher came to the filling-station. He came sidling up the driveway with a stealthy, soft-treading gait, making no noise at all with his feet on the gravel. He had an army knapsack slung over one shoulder and he was wearing an old-fashioned black jacket with large pockets. His brown corduroy trousers were tied round the knees with pieces of white string.

"Yes?" Claud asked, knowing very well who he was.

"Rodent operative." His small dark eyes moved swiftly over the premises.

"The ratcatcher?"

"That's me."

The man was lean and brown with a sharp face and two long sulphur-coloured teeth that protruded from the upper jaw, overlapping the lower lip, pressing it inward. The ears were thin and pointed and set far back on the head, near the nape of the neck. The eyes were almost black but when they looked at you there was a flash of yellow somewhere inside them.

"You've come very quick."

"Special orders from the Health Officer."

"And now you're going to catch all the rats?"

"Yep."

The kind of dark furtive eyes he had were those of an animal that lives its life peering out cautiously and forever from a hole in the ground.

"How are you going to catch em?"

"Ah-h-h," the ratman said darkly. "That's all accordin to where they is."

"Trap em, I suppose."

"Trap em," he cried, disgusted. "You won't catch many rats that way! Rats isn't rabbits you know."

He held his face up high, sniffing the air with a nose that twitched perceptibly from side to side.

"No," he said, scornfully. "Trappin's no way to catch a rat. Rats is clever, let me tell you that. If you want to catch em, you got to know em. You got to know rats on this job."

I could see Claud staring at him with a certain fascination.

"Their more clever'n dogs, rats is."

"Get away."

"You know what they do? They watch you! All the time you're going round preparing to catch em, they're sitting quietly in dark places, watchin you." The man crouched, stretching his stringy neck far forward.

Who is the monster?

FOCUS

- To consider the relationship between Victor and the monster in the modern imagination.

Essay title

'Frankenstein has become the monster.' What relevance does this statement have for us in the twenty-first century?

- To explore why the name 'Frankenstein' has become the monster's name you need to consider how the story has been changed or reinterpreted in different ways and why.

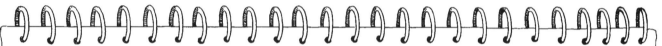

Planning

Stage 1: You could begin by considering how views of 'the monster' have changed and suggest reasons for this. For example:

a. **How is he portrayed by Mary Shelley in the novel?**

First, he is never given a name and remains the object of fear. Second, while the monster is originally good, he becomes evil (albeit as a result of his treatment) and shows no feelings of remorse for his actions, only sorrow at his own condition. He is also presented as intelligent and articulate.

b. **How is he portrayed in the modern imagination? (e.g. film versions of Frankenstein)?**

First, he is given a name (i.e. 'Frankenstein'). This is important because it makes him more human and allows him to be viewed sympathetically. Second, he is usually perceived as a victim to be pitied, rather than scorned. He is often inarticulate and vulnerable, despite his strength.

Stage 2: Consider how views of Victor Frankenstein have changed.

a. **How is he portrayed by Mary Shelley in the novel?**

First, he is portrayed as idealistic with good intentions – foolhardy, troubled, arrogant even, but not evil. Second, it is the attempt to 'play God' which is condemned, rather than Victor himself. He is seen in a more sympathetic light than the monster.

b. **How is he portrayed in the modern imagination? (Again, think about films, adverts, cartoons etc.)**

First, there is a greater emphasis on Victor's obsession leading to madness – the 'mad scientist'. Second, he is usually portrayed as dangerous and sometimes as evil or power-crazy. There is a shift of sympathy from Victor to the monster.

Stage 3: Conclude by talking about how the *Frankenstein* story has become a modern myth; how it is a warning regarding modern scientific developments. Summarise how Victor has changed and how the monster, now called 'Frankenstein', is the 'monstrous' result of science. Also, mention modern attitudes to disability – do these have an impact?

 © Folens (copiable page)

Useful questions

1. **Victor's arrogance is his downfall. Do you agree or can his downfall be attributed to other factors too?**
   Examine at least three examples in the novel to make your point.

OR

2. **Elizabeth is a poorly constructed character, Justine is more interesting. Is this true?**
   Compare the natures and actions of both characters.

3. **All the characters in the novel reject the monster.**
   Consider the truth of this statement, several characters' responses to the monster and their significance.

OR

4. **Do you think the framework of the novel helps or hinders the telling of the story?**
   In your answer, consider what the framework is, its complexity and purpose.

5. **Mary Shelley draws on literature from the past and scientific ideas of the time to make her points. Furthermore, her novel still has relevance for us today. Do you agree?**
   Refer to specific examples in the novel to support your comments.

OR

6. **How does the novel depict 'the alien'? What is the author telling us? In what way is this a theme in modern science fiction?**
   In your answer, refer to a modern science-fiction novel as well as *Frankenstein*.

7. **Mary Shelley's mother, Mary Wollstonecraft, seemed to have a greater understanding of women's condition than her daughter.**
   Decide whether or not you agree with this comment and refer to *Frankenstein* and any other relevant writing of the time.

OR

8. **Time and again, *Frankenstein* has been reinterpreted. It is a story that will not go away.**
   Consider the appeal of the story and refer to specific examples of its retelling and the purpose of these.

Uncertainty

FOCUS

- To write an answer in which you question the reliability of the events and descriptions presented in 'The Black Cat'.

Essay title

How does the story convey a sense of **uncertainty**, so that we are not sure what to believe in 'The Black Cat'?

Before you begin: remember the key word 'uncertainty' and keep this in mind when writing your answer.

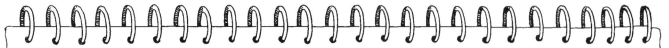

Planning

Stage 1: You could begin by pointing out that 'The Black Cat' is a story of the supernatural and, if we look closely, we can see that it has certain features that make us question what we are being told.

Stage 2: Identify as many areas of uncertainty in the story as you can. For example (and most importantly):

a. The unreliability of the narrator, particularly in the opening paragraph, in which he declares himself 'not mad' but tells us a story of his madness.

   You should also consider the following:

b. From whose point of view is the story told? What does this mean?

c. What are the descriptions of the supernatural like? Reliable? Exaggerated? Could they take place in the narrator's mind? (Give examples, such as the descriptions of Pluto before and after the narrator's decline and the presence of the 'other' cat. Is this a real cat or not?)

d. The lack of information about the character's histories.

e. The lack of information (such as names) about the setting.

Stage 3: List other points related to the events and tone (mood) of the story.

Stage 4: Conclude by referring to the title above, summing up the uncertain elements – in particular, the mixture of confusion and clarity the narrator demonstrates.

Finally, you could comment on whether or not all supernatural stories are, by definition, meant to be untrustworthy.

         © Folens (copiable page)

Useful questions

1. **How does Edgar Allan Poe create an atmosphere of fear and horror in the story?**
   Consider the use of language as well as character and setting.

OR

2. **The narrator's wife is not a real character, only a symbol. Do you think this is true?**
   In your answer, refer to other symbols in the novel to make your points.

3. **From the beginning we know that the outcome of the story will be sinister.**
   In your answer, discuss how the narrator seems unable to help himself, as well as the atmosphere of the story.

OR

4. **What does the black cat represent in the story?**
   Discuss a range of possibilities in your answer.

5. **What features of 'The Black Cat' share similarities with modern tales of fantasy and imagination?**
   Refer to a modern text as well as 'The Black Cat' to make your points.

OR

6. **It has been said that Edgar Allan Poe is the father of the detective novel. What features of 'The Black Cat' support this?**
   Refer to a detective novel or story written in the twentieth century in your answer.

7. **The narrator's wife tolerates a great deal from her husband and remains uncomplaining. How would we regard such a character in a novel written today?**
   In your answer, refer to more than one modern novel or story you know.

OR

8. **In the eighteenth and nineteenth centuries, the Gothic was popular in literature and other works of art. 'The Black Cat' can be described as a Gothic tale. Explain why.**
   In your answer, refer to another story by Edgar Allan Poe as well as 'The Black Cat', or other examples of the Gothic in works of art.

Selected answers

Who says? (Page 22)

1. Alphonse Frankenstein in a letter to Victor on discovering the body of William. (Chapter 7)
2. Robert Walton in a letter to his sister on seeing the monster travelling across the ice. (Letter 4)
3. Justine to Elizabeth about her condemnation as a murderer. (Chapter 8)
4. The monster recounting to Victor the realisation of his ugliness and lack of identity. (Chapter 15)
5. Victor recounting to Robert Walton how he found solace in beautiful landscapes. (Chapter 10)
6. Victor recounting to Robert Walton the horror of discovering what he had created. (Chapter 5)

Telling the story 2 (Page 25)

1. b. Robert Walton in a letter to his sister, explaining that he will record Victor's story as it is told to him. (Letter 4)
   c. Victor requesting that Robert Walton kills the monster, if he himself should die. Robert Walton has recorded this as part of Victor's story. (Chapter 24)
   d. Elizabeth is speaking in a letter to Victor who is recounting this to Robert Walton as part of his story. Robert Walton has recorded this. (Chapter 22)
   e. Victor telling Robert Walton about his work. Robert Walton has recorded it. (Chapter 5)

Key quotations (Page 41)

2 a. This occurs in the opening paragraph of 'The Black Cat' and is important because of its irony: the narrator tells us he is not mad, recounts his story lucidly, but it is a story of his decline into madness. It also questions whether or not the narrator is reliable.
   b. This occurs at the beginning of the story. Its importance lies in its depiction of the narrator as gentle and mild-mannered in contrast to the change he undergoes.
   c. This occurs early in the story and makes reference to Pluto. The superstition relating to black cats and witches is important in the light of what happens subsequently in the story.

The narrative voice (Page 42)

1. a. first person
   b. in the story
   c. from a single point of view
   d. sometimes exaggerates (within the context of the Gothic novel)
   e. believes the story
   f. trick question! Poe is playing with the reader. The narrator invites us to believe him, but in the opening paragraph says that he would be 'mad' to expect us to.
2. Students can decide for themselves, but the evidence in a. to f. suggests that the voice is ambiguous.

Climaxes (Page 45)

1. a. The narrator hangs Pluto (minor climax).
   b. The discovery of the corpse and the cat (main climax).
   c. The narrator claims to see the image of a 'gigantic' cat (minor climax).
   d. The narrator is about to kill his wife (minor climax).
   e. The narrator cuts out Pluto's eye (minor climax).